Skin

Cassie Mayer

Heinemann Library
Chicago, Illinois

Photo research by Tracy Cummins and Erica Newbery
Designed by Jo Hinton-Malivoire
Printed and bound in China by South China Printing Company
10 09 08 07 06
10 9 8 7 6 5 4 3 2 1

Library of Congress Cataloging-in-Publication Data
Mayer, Cassie.
  Skin / Cassie Mayer.
      p. cm. -- (Body coverings)
  Includes bibliographical references and index.
  ISBN 1-4034-8373-6 (hc) -- ISBN 1-4034-8379-5 (pb)
  1. Skin--Juvenile literature. I. Title.
  QL941.M39 2006
  573.5--dc22
                          2005036087

Acknowledgments
The author and publisher are grateful to the following for permission to reproduce copyright material:
Corbis pp. **5** (rhino, Royalty Free), **7** and **8** (Lynda Richardson), **12** (Ralph A. Clevenger), **13** and **14** (Daniel J. Cox), **15** and **16** (Joe McDonald), **20** (Kevin Dodge), **23** (rhino, Royalty Free), **23** (scales and snake, Joe McDonald), **23** (manatee, Daniel J. Cox); FLPA pp. **11** and **12** (Minden Pictures), **22** (iguana); Getty Images pp. **6** (Balfour), **9** and **10** (Parfitt), **17** and **18** (Wolfe); Getty Images/Digital Vision pp. **4** (kingfisher and leopard), **22** (hippo), Getty Images/PhotoDisc p. **4** (snail and lizard); Science Photo Library p. **22** (sweat, Dick Luria).

Cover image of elephant skin reproduced with permission of Wyman/Getty Images. Back cover image of a frog reproduced with permission of Wolfe/Getty Images.

Every effort has been made to contact copyright holders of any material reproduced in this book.
Any omissions will be rectified in subsequent printings if notice is given to the publisher.

Contents

Body Coverings 4

Types of Skin 6

Your Own Skin 19

Fun Skin Facts. 22

Picture Glossary 23

Index 24

feathers

shell

scales

fur

Animals have body coverings.
Body coverings protect animals.

skin

Skin is a body covering.
Animals have skin.

There are many types of skin.

Skin can be wet.
What animal is this?

This animal is a salamander.
It breathes through its skin.

Skin can be dry.
What animal is this?

This animal is an elephant.
Its skin has wrinkles.

Skin can be smooth.
What animal is this?

This animal is a dolphin.
Its skin helps it swim fast.

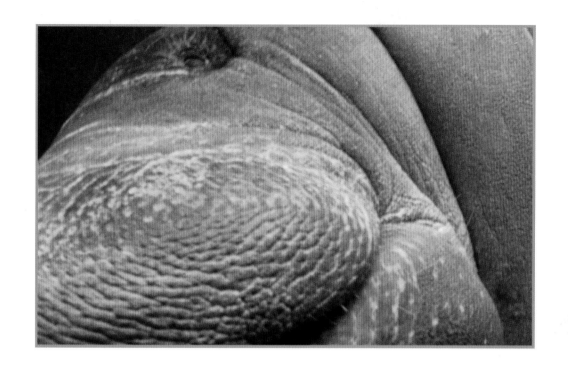

Skin can be rough.
What animal is this?

This animal is a manatee.
Its skin is waterproof.

Skin can be scaly.
What animal is this?

This animal is a snake.
It sheds its skin.

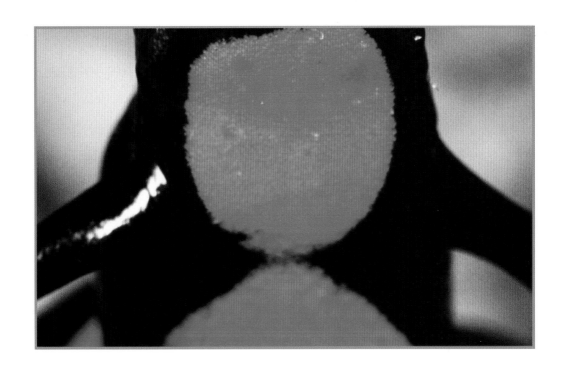

Skin can be bright colors.
What animal is this?

This animal is a poison-dart frog.
Its skin says "Danger!"

Do you have skin?

Yes, you have skin!

What is your skin like?

Fun Skin Facts

Humans and other animals sweat through their skin. Sweating keeps them cool.

Iguanas have skin that keeps their body from drying out.

Hippos have a built-in sunscreen. Their body makes a liquid that protects their skin.

Picture Glossary

 **scaly** covered in scales

 **shed** to take off

 **skin** a type of body covering

 **waterproof** not changed by water

Index

body covering,
   4, 5
dolphin, 11, 12
elephant, 9, 10
manatee, 13, 14

poison-dart frog,
   17, 18
salamander, 7, 8
snake, 15, 16

Note to Parents and Teachers

In this book, children explore characteristics of skin and are introduced to a variety of animals that use this covering for protection. Visual clues and the repetitive question, "What animal is this?" engage children by providing a predictable structure from which to learn new information. The text has been chosen with the advice of a literacy expert to enable beginning readers success while reading independently or with moderate support. Scientists were consulted to provide both interesting and accurate content.

The book ends with an open-ended question that asks children to relate the material to their lives. Use this question as a writing or discussion prompt to encourage creative thinking and assess comprehension. You can also support children's nonfiction literacy skills by helping them to use the table of contents, picture glossary, and index.